HOW TO.

BUY A HOUSE

BY PROPERTY STRATEGIST

Because of the dynamic nature of the internet, any websites used in this book may have changed since publication and may no longer be valid.

www.propertystrat.co.uk

Let us not become weary in doing good, for at the proper time we will reap a harvest if we do not give up.

(Galatians 6:9)

CONTENTS

PROLOGUE...1

WHY PROPERTY?...3

WHAT'S NEEDED & CREDIT.....................................6

GET A MORTGAGE IN PRINCIPLE............................9

CAN I AFFORD THIS PROPERTY?...........................11

MAKING AN OFFER...13

SOLICITORS: WHAT DO THEY DO?.........................16

TIPS TO SPEED UP THE BUYING PROCESS...........19

TO CONCLUDE..21

GLOSSARY...23

PROLOGUE

We as the Property Strategists are a team of three boys from South London (Akin, Goke and Kenny) who have been investing in property since 2014. We decided to come together and document our journey for like-minded young individuals wanting to start their journey in property as well. We provide gems on different ways to make money in property that often aren't taught. Our aim is to empower a young hungry generation with all the tools needed to win in property.

1

WHY PROPERTY?

When considering property investment, it's important to begin with the basics and to understand how this type of profitable investment can build your asset portfolio.

Many would like to experience the "breakthrough" in life, whether it is a new job with a great salary, an opportunity to experience your deepest desires or alternatively creating a novel idea in the hope for financial freedom. Investing in property does not require a breakthrough of niche ideas and frankly, you do not need to conjure up a platform such as Facebook to build your asset column. You can invest in property today without significant background knowledge and reap the benefits for years to come.

For example, today I may invest in a property in the midlands for £60,000. In 10 years' time, the same property has increased in value and is worth up to £100,000. This means my investment 10 years ago has brought in £40,000 in profit. Arguably, I have made a profit without requiring extensive knowledge or skills I would require for investing in stocks, bonds, shares or ETIs.

"INVESTING IN PROPERTY DOES NOT REQUIRE A BREAKTHROUGH OF NICHE IDEAS."

Besides the benefits of building your streams of income, investing in a property transitions you into what is known as generational wealth.

How many of you were passed down a property from your wealthy parents or affluent relatives? The likelihood is many of you (like us) were not handed a pair of keys to a new home, with a shiny front door, acres of back garden, and a driveway for the Benz! But you can be the family member who creates this wealth for the generation to come. This is why it is imperative to invest in properties as soon as you can. By investing in properties today, you can begin the foundation of a lasting legacy of wealth for the future generations.

Lastly, investing in property can be a great way to generate a passive source of income. All of us dream of acquiring additional sources of income outside our 9 to 5 day jobs.

For example, in a buy-to-let investment, you can benefit from what is called *passive income* by receiving rent paid to you by a tenant. We say passive because all being well, whether you are working or not, the house is generating you money through the rent you receive. The level of passivity is dependent on whether you are managing the property yourself or paying someone to complete this on your behalf. This can help with building a rainy day fund and the provision of a personal maintenance fund for comfortable living.

2

WHAT'S NEEDED & CREDIT

Before delving deeper into the essentials for property investment, here are some crucial points you should be familiar with prior to your big purchase.

Typically, when buying a property, you will be requested either by your lender or broker to provide a minimum of 3 months bank statements and pay slips. They will review your expenditure every month and confirm you have consistent income paid into your bank account over a period. This is to ensure you are not a money launderer, you are reliable and can be trusted to pay off the monthly mortgage re-payments. It is key to note the requirements of some lenders may differ.

"EVEN IF YOU HAVE DOUBLE THE DEPOSIT REQUIRED FOR A PROPERTY, YOU CAN STILL BE REFUSED FUNDS IF YOUR CREDIT HISTORY IS UNSATISFACTORY."

Secondly, knowing the purpose of investment will determine the type of mortgage to go for and the deposit you will need to purchase. For example, should you wish to buy a property for the intention of renting it out to tenants, you may be in need of a buy-to-let mortgage. This usually requires a deposit of 25% of the total value of the property. In contrast, should you wish to buy a property to live in, you will be in need of a residential mortgage (which usually requires 10%). Using figures, a property worth £100,000 will require a residential mortgage and a deposit of £10,000 should you wish to live in it. By contrast, should you wish to rent out a property, you will need a buy-to-let mortgage and £25,000 deposit.

Understanding your credit history is equally as important when purchasing a property. Simply put, credit is the ability to borrow money, goods or services with the understanding you must pay the lender back later. This is vital as a lender will review your history of borrowing through a credit report and determine whether you are reliable enough to be granted funds. You can obtain your credit report using various websites such as Experian, Equifax and Noddle. Even if you have double the deposit required for a property, you can still be refused funds if your credit history is unsatisfactory. Please note, advice on improving credit should be sought after online or through a qualified financial advisor.

3.

GET A MORTGAGE IN PRINCIPLE

B uying a house involves a collection of stages coming together. The first stage is to get a mortgage in principle (MIP) from a lender of your choosing or from those available to you. A MIP is also known as a decision in principle or agreement in principle. A MIP is a statement from your lender identifying how much they will be willing to give you providing all the information you have delivered to your broker is accurate. You can do this by going either to a mortgage broker or directly to a bank of your choice. A MIP is based on the data extracted from your income. Lenders generally provide you with 4-5x your annual salary, taking your outgoings and credit into account.

You should be able to get a MIP for free and typically within a few minutes. It will generally be valid between 60-90 days, after which, a new MIP will need to be attained should you still wish to purchase a property. However, by no means does a MIP commit you to follow through with a purchase.

"THIS COULD BE THE EDGE YOU NEED OVER ANOTHER BUYER."

Having an MIP in place can also be beneficial in other ways. It can be used as a means to reassure sellers that you've made progress with acquiring a mortgage, thus making you more trustworthy and reliable. This could be the edge you need over another buyer in helping a seller choose you over somebody else.

It's important to note as well that acquiring a MIP may leave footprints on your credit file, so be sure to check whether your lender will perform a soft search or a hard search. In a soft search, although searches are recorded, lenders are unable to see them. This means soft searches will not impact your credit score. In contrast, hard searches are recorded, meaning lenders are able to see that you've applied for credit before.

4.

CAN I AFFORD THIS PROPERTY?

L ike most people in the world, before buying a property, you probably have an idea of a dream home you would love to live in. However, after understanding how mortgages work, you have an idea of what you are allowed to borrow and ultimately the type of property you can afford.

Attaining a MIP will be the clearest indication of your affordability. As previously stated, a MIP is a statement from a lender to show how much you can borrow. This will help eliminate properties outside of your budget and open your eyes to properties available within your financial plan.

"A MIP WILL BE THE CLEAREST INDICATION OF YOUR AFFORDABILITY."

11

Once you have established how much you can afford, the next step is finding a property that fits within your budget. The two main websites for property searches are www.rightmove.co.uk and www.zoopla.co.uk. With these websites, you can apply filters to single out properties by location, size, pricing, and various other features. Also note that any properties worth more than £125,000 will legally require you to pay Stamp Duty. However, if you're a first-time buyer in England or Northern Ireland, you will pay no Stamp Duty on properties worth up to £300,000! So it is important to also factor in Stamp Duty when looking at your affordability.

5.

MAKING AN OFFER

_____

W hen you find the property you've been looking for, the next step is making an offer. However, before making an offer, it's useful going through these steps to ensure the offer you make is inclusive of all the possible factors.

It's important to understand why the owner is selling the property, as this may have an impact on the offer you put forward or which offer is accepted. For example, if the seller is looking for an urgent sale, offering under-market value may be welcomed. In contrast, if the seller isn't in a rush to sell, this same offer may have a negative effect on your offer being accepted. So, having an understanding of why the property is being sold can be advantageous.

"JUST BECAUSE A PROPERTY IS LISTED AT £100K DOESN'T MEAN IT'S ACTUALLY WORTH IT!"

Another important step before buying a property is research. Just because a property is listed at £100k doesn't mean it's actually worth it! Before making an offer, use all the resources available to make an informed decision. Websites like Rightmove, Zoopla and Land Registry can give you similar properties sold nearby and how much they sold for. If you're lucky, you can find a nearby property sold within the same year to give you a better idea of what your property is actually worth.

Once an offer has been made, your lender will send out a qualified surveyor to perform a survey on the property you wish to purchase. The three basic types of surveys are as follows:

1. **RICS Home Conditions Report** - Looks at any urgent defects, the general property condition and potential legal issues. (£250-£550)

2. **RICS Homebuyers Report** - Includes all the services from a conditions report and an insurance reinstatement value. (£400-£900)

3. **RICS Building Survey -** These are more extensive and include inspection behind walls, between floors and above ceilings. It will give you an estimate on how much the repairs will cost and the repercussions of not repairing them. (£600-£1400)

Ultimately, the role of a surveyor is to inspect the property with great detail to ensure the price listed reflects the actual asking price from the lender. This can create big issues when the surveyor values the property lower than the asking price. In such situations, this may mean you as the buyer will need to go back to the seller and ask them to reduce their price or fork out the difference yourself! Also note, for instances when you have paid for a surveyor and the property is valued lower than the asking price, you may not be entitled to a refund (should you wish to pull out of the purchase). So please read the terms of the agreement before going forward.

6.

SOLICITORS: WHAT DO THEY DO?

When you've found a house, agreed on a mortgage in principle and started to go through a full mortgage application, you'll need to find a solicitor. The main role of a solicitor in purchasing a property is to transfer the legal ownership of the property from the seller to the buyer. Other things they're tasked with are to review the mortgage offer and to ensure you're in the loop with everything you need to know and order searches on your behalf (flood risk, water authority, title and environmental searches); they will also receive the deposit from you when ready for the exchanging on contracts. Typically, solicitors can cost anywhere from £1000-2000 for a standard purchase; however, this may vary depending on the type of property.

"BOTH PARTIES ARE LEGALLY BOUND TO FINALISE THE SALE/PURCHASE."

An *Exchange of Contracts* is the point at which both parties are legally bound to finalise the sale/purchase on the agreed completion date. That means the solicitors of both the buyer and the seller have written up and agreed to the terms of the contracts on your behalf and have set a date for all dealings to be complete. This is also the stage at which the buyers solicitor pays a **non refundable** deposit to the seller. Using the example from Chapter 2, the property worth £100,000 will mean your solicitor must send a deposit of £10,000 or £25,000 for the respective mortgage you require *i.e.* residential or buy-to-let.

Completion is the date that a buyer will be legally allowed to move into the property. It's also the date by which the buyers solicitor must transfer all the remaining funds to the seller. However, for completion, all processes must be finalised. This means the survey would have come back without any detrimental property defects, the mortgage would have been agreed and delivered and the property searches would have come back without blemish *e.g.* without a default. Once a completion date is agreed, an application is made on your behalf to the Land Registry to change the title deed of the property to your name as the buyer.

7.

TIPS TO SPEED UP THE BUYING PROCESS

A t this point, we would have gone over all the steps involved in buying a property. However, the length of this process can vary from a matter of weeks to a number of months, depending on a variety of factors. The good news is there are steps you can take that can potentially speed up this process.

4 Ways to Improve Your Credit Score

1. Register on the Electoral Roll
2. Pay off your debt
3. Join a credit scoring agency *e.g.*, Equifax
4. Build a credit history

Check your credit file! It's important to check your credit file before starting the process of buying a house as this allows you to see it before lenders do. Therefore you can identify any errors and rectify them before making a mortgage application.

"CHECK YOUR CREDIT FILE!"

Use an experienced mortgage broker! A good and experienced broker will match your personal circumstances to the right mortgage lender and product. This will increase your likelihood of getting a mortgage offer. Make sure you are transparent with your broker during the application so they can better match you with lenders that will lend to you. Failing to do so can greatly delay the process if new discoveries are found that could have been disclosed earlier.

Pick a really good solicitor! This is important because you want a solicitor who will carry out the conveyancing process with speed and efficiency. It is important to get referrals and also read reviews to ensure you have a reputable solicitor.

Keep in regular contact with your broker and solicitor for updates. This allows you to make sure everyone is doing whatever is in their control in order to get the purchase over the line, and for once, it's okay to be annoying! Furthermore, provide everything requested as quickly as possible. You do not want to be the reason there is a delay, so do the bits that are within your control as quickly as possible. We live in a generation where technology has evolved, so take advantage and make use of the apps out there that can quicken the process (such as PDF scanners).

8.

TO CONCLUDE

B y this point, you understand the main processes involved in purchasing a property. The initial step was to get a mortgage in principle from a lender to allow you to know the type of properties you can afford. This is an important step because this ultimately can determine the type of property you get, *e.g.*, a flat or a detached house, and in some cases, the location of your property, *e.g.* properties tend to be cheaper in the midlands than in London.

Next was to make an informed offer on the property you're looking at. This included doing research using all the tools and websites available to give you a better idea of the actual price of the property listed. Your lender will then arrange for a surveyor to come and give an even more detailed inspection of the property in question. This will then determine the lender's valuation of the property and ultimately decide how much they can lend you for the purchase of that property.

A solicitor comes into play by acting as an intercessor to arrange the exchanging of contracts, conduct property

21

searches, and address any enquiries. When everything comes back okay, the solicitor arranges the completion of the purchase. After completion, the property is yours! You can now move in and start your property journey!

THE 10 STEPS OF BUYING A HOUSE

Establish a budget

Get a MIP

Make an offer

Start mortgage application

Instruct a solicitor

Property survey

Mortgage offer received

Contracts exchanged

Deposit Paid

COMPLETION

GLOSSARY

Asset
Something of monetary value than an individual or company owns, benefits from, or has use of, in generating income.

Credit
The ability to borrow money, goods or services with the understanding to pay them back later.

Completion
The legal move-in date; the seller leaves the property and the buyer is given the keys to move in.

Conveyancing
The transfer of legal ownership/title of a property from one party to another

Exchange of Contracts
The point at which both parties are legally bound to finalise the sale/purchase of a property on the agreed completion date.

Hard Search
A search used by companies to show your full credit history. This search leaves a mark on your credit file.

Mortgage
A loan taken out to buy a property.

Buy-To-Let Mortgage
A mortgage with the intention of renting it out, typically requiring a larger deposit of 25% of the property value.

Residential Mortgage
A mortgage with the intention to live in, typically requiring a deposit of 10% of the property value.

Mortgage in Principle (MIP)
A statement from the lender to say how much you'll be able to lend, provided the information you've given is accurate.

Passive Income
An income that requires little to no effort to earn and maintain.

RICS
Royal Institute of Chartered Surveyors. A professional body that promotes and enforces the highest professional standards in the development of land, property, infrastructure and construction.

Soft Search
A search made on your credit file that will not affect your credit score.

Stamp Duty
Tax paid when purchasing a residential property. It is based on increasing portions of the property value on any amount over £125,000.

Survey
A detailed inspection of the condition of a property.

Title Deed
Paper documents that show the chain of ownership for land and property.

Printed in Great Britain
by Amazon